Wilhelm von Kaulbach, Erwin Förster

**Schiller Gallery**

Wilhelm von Kaulbach, Erwin Förster

**Schiller Gallery**

ISBN/EAN: 9783337330989

Printed in Europe, USA, Canada, Australia, Japan

Cover: Foto ©Thomas Meinert / pixelio.de

More available books at **www.hansebooks.com**

SCHILLER

# SCHILLER-GALLERY.

FROM THE ORIGINAL DRAWINGS

OF

## WILLIAM KAULBACH,

C. JAEGER, A. MUELLER, TH. PIXIS, R. BEYSCHLAG,
W. LINDENSCHMIT.

WITH EXPLANATORY TEXT BY E. FOERSTER.

# PREFACE.

When the masterly pencil of *William Kaulbach* offered us his ideal conceptions of the female characters of *Goethe;* and thereby, as it were, embodied the thoughts of the poet, — the public received the precious gift not only with general sympathy; but with loud acclamation. The art of antiquity revealed the high denizens of Olympus—that of the middle-ages, the Saints and Martyrs of the Christian church— even the inexplicable Trinity—and thereby aroused the faithful to adoration,— in the same manner has *Kaulbach* achieved a conquest in the field of modern German art, which seems destined to produce magnificent fruits. During the last century Germany produced men, whose high intellectual flights, whose words of thunder awakened the people from that lamentable state of lethargy, which succeeded the terrible religious wars of that country. These illustrious men were inspired with the one great sentiment:

> "We will be a united People, in the bonds of true brotherhood."

1

Certainly these master-minds have left a treasure, the like no other nation possesses—a legacy, sacred and precious, and yet accessible to every one, anxious for its possession. It is by no means a rare occurrence that the productions of great men have long remained to the multitude an unexplained mystery; which to unravel is the office of the twin-sisters: "Science and Art." Gladly did the publisher of the *Goethe-Gallery* offer the latter a welcome hand, in agreeing to publish an illustration to the works of that poet, whom the Germans above all regard as a truly national one—to bring his lofty thoughts again nearer home to us, in unfolding to our wondering eyes, now the magnificent plains of Elysium; and again the homely towns, and simple family-life of the German people. The more arduous the task appeared to clothe the sublime ideals of this poet in visible forms; manifesting thereby their intrinsic value—to make them generally understood—great and laudable as such an object ever must be—it was impossible to entrust to one single hand the execution, and hence several artists were invited to cooperate. It was not only requisite to show the female characters of *Schiller* in special and characteristic scenes—it was necessary to produce to the most important passages of his poems, his dramatic and prose works, illustrations in the best and highest sense of the word.

The publisher inviting younger artists to cooperate in the execution of the work, afforded them an excellent opportunity to compete for the prize; and to

profit by the example of the great master of the
*Goethe-Gallery*, to whom this work is also in some
measure indebted. Different as the works of *Goethe*
and *Schiller* are the one from the other—they belong
nevertheless indivisibly together, and supplement
each other. Thus it is contemplated that the *Schiller-
Gallery*, not only in its external appearance, but in
real value—shall be the worthy sister of the female
characters of *Goethe*. The publisher flatters himself
to offer the public a great national work,—an imperish-
able memorial of the great poet—who in view of the
high calling of the artist thus exclaimed:

> "Modestly arisen from clay or stone—
> Creative Art embraces in silent conquest
> The immeasurable region of the mind!
> What in the field of knowledge is discovered—
> Is yours,—for you it is conquered.
> The treasures heaped up by the thinker,
> Will he enjoy only when embraced by you,
> When his science, ripened into beauty,
> Becomes ennobled to a work of art!"

# Maria Stuart.

MARIA STUART

# MARIA STUART.

History will always regard Elizabeth the greatest
of English Queens.—During her reign the national
church was established, which prevented the sangui-
nary religious conflicts raging on the continent of
Europe. She received favorably those who had escaped persecution in France and Holland; encouraged
these refugees, and laid the foundation to the great-
ness of English industry. From the wrecks of the
Spanish Armada arose the mighty fleet of England,
—and in Elizabeth's time the first English colonies
were established in America. Admiring the great
mind which achieved these memorable things,—we
are on the other hand compelled to turn aside from
the means employed,—and are constrained to confess:
"that Elizabeth possessing the masculine virtues of
rulers, inherited the blemishes only of her own sex."
To portray such a female, and to exhibit a picture,
in which majesty, power, and concern for the people,
were closely associated with malice, revenge, and a
contemptible jealousy,—this was a task which only
men like Schiller could accomplish. Yet it was of

scarcely less difficulty to give a visible picture of
such an extraordinary lady—and to achieve this, perhaps no one possessed better qualifications than
William Kaulbach.—The lofty brow of Elizabeth
bespeaks a mind capable to change the aspect of
two hemispheres,—eyes which seemed to read the
most secret thoughts of others, and discern by a
single glance if any one in her presence was an
opponent, or a willing instrument to further her plans.
Her firmly closed lips reveal determination and seve-
rity in judging others. This figure is every inch a
Queen—and more than her splendid attire, this proud
bearing at once announces: "The powerful occupant
of England's throne."—But the artist has also shown
us the purely human side of the character of this
great Queen; and selected the moment when the
unfortunate Maria Stuart—after vainly endeavouring
to move the heart of her enemy—exclaimed in impo-
tent rage:

> "The noble-hearted Britons,
> Are shamefully deceived by a wary juggler."

Such language Elizabeth had never heard before.
The vain praise of Leicester resounded yet in her ears:

> "Never were you for a victory of beauty
> Better equipped than even now—"

Conscious of her triumph, she had entered the
park, and here a defenceless woman had insulted her.
Speechless, she presses her right hand upon her
heart, as if a dagger's point had pierced it—and
with her left—as if bent upon revenge—she seizes

a rose-tree, and kills a flower before its bloom. In
this state of rage she disregards her own pain and
seems unmindful of her favourite falcon, which fright-
ened flutters at her feet. But how appears Mary?
She is not a meek suppliant, but the innocent con-
demned woman, in whom again the memory of her
own majesty is aroused; and who might well ex-
claim:

> "If justice ruled—you would be at my feet
> For I am your rightful Queen!"

This sentiment seems visible in the flaming eye;
and pointing to herself, she raises her left hand
indignantly over Elizabeth. The ancient rancour
nestled in her breast has burst its fetters; and triumph-
ing for the moment over her rival, she laughs at
her personal danger, and is deaf to the wise counsel
of her trusty attendant—nor does she regard the
secret signs of honest Shrewsbury,—whose last ray
of hope disappears in sight of the violent behaviour
of the dethroned Queen of Scotland. The contrast
between the silent rage on the one side—and the
outbreak of long suppressed hatred on the other—
could have hardly been better represented than in
this master-piece of Kaulbach. Yet whilst we here
recognise in Elizabeth the picture of offended pride,
and thirst for swift revenge—and the noble anger
of Mary; together with the faithful attachment of
the aged nurse,—we are forcibly struck by the miser-
able figure of the Earl of Leicester. He, the para-
mour of two Princesses—he, who betrayed beauty,

2

in order to preserve power—here he stands, like a
boy who, caught in an evil act, dares not venture to
raise his eyes. This momentous scene in which a
human being sees the last ray of hope vanish—is
enclosed with the sombre park, and the strong castle
of Fotheringhay is towering over the tops of the
trees. They give a finish to the sublime quietude
and simplicity, and afford a sure test of genuine art.

# The Maid of Orleans.

JOAN OF ARC

# THE MAID OF ORLEANS.

There have been at all times, and in all countries females, who in the wars of their native land, either took a leading part, or at least assisted in the deadly strife. The daughters of Spain and the Tyrol fought at the side of their countrymen. Prohaska fell fighting in the corps of Luetzow—and during the great war in America, women of the North entered the ranks of the army. We may, however, affirm that none of all heroines, has been more surrounded with the splendor of romantic chivalry, than Joan d'Arc --remarkable even in the most prosaic accounts of her history. Yet notwithstanding this, a long time elapsed ere the well deserved crown of immortality was offered to the maiden. France left it to an Englishman, to sing the praises of the foe of his own nation—nay more, one of the greatest poets of France did not hesitate to ridicule the bold heroism of Joan. It was reserved for Schiller to arouse again the slumbering enthusiasm in behalf of the Maid of Orleans by a magnificent poem. Since then art also has erected numerous monuments in honour of the Maid. Most of them·

however, represent Joan either on the height of fortune,—or else portray the terrible end, which fanaticism, enmity, and superstition had prepared for her. Different from these is Kaulbach's picture—who, giving us the commencement of Joan's heroic career, affords us, at the same time, the key to this mysterious phenomenon. A peaceful shepherdess, far removed from scenes of strife and battle, places herself at the head of the desponding army—and in the hour when all seemed lost—leads them to victory, and restores to the king his lost crown. Joan acknowledged herself to be merely the instrument of heaven; and in that sense, both poet and artist represent her. Only the command from on high could steel the arm of the feeble maid,—from above she received, instead of the shepherd's staff—a two-edged sword. Only the will of heaven induced her to renounce the quiet joys of married life, to banish pity from her bosom, and love from her heart. Thrice did the blessed virgin appear to her under the sacred oak at Dom Remi, and, when Joan still doubting her strength hesitated to execute the high behest, reveal herself as the Queen of heaven; giving her the banner which she was to carry in front of the victorious army. It is still night, and only some feeble streaks of light in the far east announce the dawn of day. In spite of paternal warnings Joan had again spent the night under the favorite oak, when lo! a heavenly light appears, and on a golden cloud the virgin descends, and arms the maid against the foes of the

oldest throne in Christendom. In silent ecstacy the
maid kneels before the Saint, receiving the benedic-
tions of her blessed son. What charming sweetness
in the face of Mary, with what loving sympathy
she regards the Maid devoted to her service. And
Joan?—See how her countenance reflects the enthusiasm for the cause she has espoused! and yet again
the whole attitude evinces that modesty, with which
she refused every praise. Through the airy attire
we recognise the noble form and figure of the Maid
who changed the hostility of Lionel into love; and
overcame the relentless foe within the British camp,
—the Duke of Burgundy—who being reconciled and
led by her into the presence of the king exclaimed:

"Oh she can do with me whate'er she likes;
My heart is in her hands like melting wax."

# The Robbers.

THE ROBBERS

# THE ROBBERS.

(Act. IV. Scene IV.)

The artist who engaged to portray this grand scene
in the production of Schiller "The Robbers", which
he wrote in his younger years and which has often
been blamed, undertook a difficult task. He has however in our opinion acquitted himself admirably. Not
selecting the wild and romantic figures of the brigands
nor a scene with lively and varying action—he brings
only "Karl and Amalie" upon the stage at the moment when their hearts wage a fierce conflict for
their love. Outwardly all seems calm, but it is the
calmness which precedes the destructive tempest.
Amalie is earnestly examining Karl's likeness, regarding it as a talisman against the danger which threat-
ens her constancy from the attention of the stranger
count.—She refuses to believe her foreboding heart
that he whom she fears is her lover himself,—she
does not trust her eyes which in the hard and wea-
therbeaten face recognise the features of "Karl"—
nor her ear which in the words: "You weep, Amalie"
—hears his voice. How could Karl be so near and

3*

not make himself known?—Hence she refuses to look
again at the seeming resemblance so perilous to her.
She will not notice that he has entered the garden
and mournfully regards her. At no time appears
Karl Moor a greater hero than now,—nowhere is
the nobility of his soul more conspicuous than in
this scene, when he denies himself in order to spare
his pure-hearted Amalie the pain to find in her returned lover a deeply degraded being—when he for ever
renounces her love, having assured himself of her
faithfulness. This is unquestionably the heaviest punishment he receives, and he inflicts it on himself volun-
tarily. This strife within himself, this alternate feeling of pleasure and pain is well depicted in every
feature.

Notwithstanding the sombre looks, the firmly closed
lips—the Artis thas succeeded in infusing some traces
of softness. The figure of this brigand-chief appearing behind the bushes is indeed that of a hero!
Only such a one could rule the wild fellows of the
Bohemian forest,—only such a one could gain the
love of Amalie.—And, as in Jaeger's later illustrations,
so we are also in this, delighted with the admirable
finish of the whole as well as of its details. The
mild and innocent features of Amalie and the hard-
ened countenance of the Robber—her simple attire
and his costly garments—are beautifully contrasted.
We are not surprised at the heavy sword which
dangles at the Robber's side - nor at the brace of
pistols in his belt; for he is ready to depart—the

horses are near to take him away from the home of
his early youth. He cannot any longer live there
since society has cast him out and he has become its
curse. Once more he will see Amalie; once more hear
her sweet voice, reminding him of the happiness he
has lost. After this he is resolved to return to his misery
until the avenging arm of justice shall punish his mis-
deeds. The stringed instrument in the foreground re-
minds us of the beautiful thought of Schiller —that,
though the heart may resist words, — music and song
are irresistable. Not the complaint for the absent one,
not even the words of tender love could move Karl
to reveal himself: but when Amalie seizes the lute
and commences a favorite song which they in happier
times had often sung together—his strength fails him
—and he replies to her as Hector:

> "Go, dear wife, fetch me my lance,
> Let me hasten to the wild war-dance."

# DON CARLOS.

DON CARLOS

# Don Carlos.

Even at this day the mentioning of the name of
Philip II. fills us with horror; calling to mind the
bloody fields of Holland, and the smoking stakes of
Spain, by which the inquisition celebrated its seeming
triumphs. All qualities which might conduce to mak-
ing a ruler great and happy, were in this King's
possession. Power, wealth, and more, a sagacious
mind and an iron will. Little did these advantages
avail. Philip tried to keep fleeting phantoms. All
his great wealth could not purchase one faithful heart.
His intellect was checked by superstition,—and his
iron will, a perpetrator of horrid cruelties. Though
he destroyed an empire and burnt a people, his
work—unity of faith—and the exclusive dominion of
Spain in Europe, perished with him when in Sep-
tember 1598 he closed his eyes in death. A dramatic
representation of such a character was no easy task.
Our poet has accomplished it in showing us in Philip
the antagonism of the ruler and the man.—Engaged
to execute his schemes he is tortured by a terrible
suspicion concerning the Queen, his wife. Policy had

1

brought about this alliance with the former bride of
his son. This son who approaches his father with
filial love, is regarded by Philip a dangerous foe—
and consequently is disowned. The virtue of Elizabeth
which in the gardens of Aranjuez had won the King's
regard, appears now, since Alba and Domingo have
calumniated her, very questionable to him. Believing
himself deceived by his own wife, for whom alone
he preserved some human sympathy—he, a King, in
whose dominion the sun does never set—discovers
himself poorer than any of his meanest subjects.
This conflict between the ruler and the man, between
hatred and love, is the basis of this composition.
Offended pride is uppermost, and opened the gates
to actual brutality. This we notice in the expression
of the countenance, the clenched fist of Philip—a
man just now entirely the slave of wild passions,
from whom we turn our eyes with disgust. On the
other hand we are all the more attracted by the
noble, dignified appearance of Elizabeth. Hers is a
god-like head, an ideal of female beauty. She, conscious of her purity of heart and mind, looks with
contempt upon this scene. Holding and protecting
her little innocent daughter in her arms, Elizabeth
appears entirely as a mother whose duty makes her
say to her brutal husband:

> "This child at least,
> I must secure against ill-usage;"

This illustration of Jaeger's is a master-piece of
technic. How beautifully are the garments drawn;

with what care the furniture of the apartment—the
clock, the candle-sticks, and the tapestry in which
the monogram of Philip's name is woven. This royal
chamber affords us a glimpse at the magnificence
of the palace and in general at the luxury of the
XVI. century. What a careful attention to minute
details and yet what admirable harmony in the
whole composition! Notwithstanding .the agitated
scene, there is a calmness prevailing in the picture
which the Artist produced by a beautiful chiaroscuro.

# WILLIAM TELL.

WILLIAM TELL

# WILLIAM TELL.

No drama has secured to Schiller so much the affection of his nation and none has more justly designated him by the name of the first singer of liberty than "William Tell". All he desired for Germany or demanded of her he puts before her by a magnificent example. Here he praises his nation and here reproves their conduct, especially that inherited sin —"disunion". Schiller was unfortunately not spared to witness the enthusiasm kindled by his words in all Germany and urging youth and man to high deeds when nine years later his Tell was publicly performed. Yet he escaped also the painful disappointment to see his words so soon forgotten. Again and again, however, was heard the outcry: "Be united, united, united!" No public feast, no serious deliberation did pass without one or another's calling to mind these weighty words. At length an urgent desire is manifested to follow the words of the poet—a desire at last accomplished. Art has seized upon this legacy of Schiller, and Jaeger, the Artist, has furnished in the death-scene of Atting-

hausen a picture which should not be wanting any-
where; a constant monitor of: "Be united, be one!"
The composition is so clear and intelligible that an
explanation seems hardly required. Examine, however,
the powerful figure of Stauffacher, whose look war-
rants his will henceforth to think only of the liberty
of his country which the dying man has solemnly
laid to his heart. Confidently does Walter Fürst
lean upon him, whilst regarding with special sympathy the dying leader. As to young Tell, the Artist
has somewhat deviated from the text. Here the
youth is not kneeling, but stands in an almost defying
attitude. In him we recognise the heroic spirit of the
father and a worthy specimen of the rising genera-
tion, worthy representatives of their ancestors.

# THE BRIDE OF MESSINA.

5

THE BRIDE OF MESSINA

# THE BRIDE OF MESSINA.

Whilst the Religion of Christ reveals God as a loving yet severe father and thereby places the fate of man in his own hands—the Mythology of Greece makes mortals the tools and even the toys of the gods. Men cannot escape their doom whatever their conduct may be. This view which reached by Sophocles to the highest poetical sanction, Schiller also attempted to raise to validity in a drama, whose characters more suffering than acting, belong already to the Christian era. There is no doubt that Schiller perceived the difficulty of the task. He could hardly avoid the appearing of pagan figures in the train of Christianity which, though historically correct, appears to us almost as strange, as the introduction of a chorus in a modern drama. Our Poet became thus the originator of the romantic tragedy of fate which during the first two decennaries of our century made much noise, but ultimately degenerated in such a manner, that Platen chastised its pretensions with bitter irony. Our Artist selected the passage from Don Manuel's tale about finding his Bride:

5*

"The hunting-spear ready to throw—,
She, however, gazed with her large eyes beseechingly
At me!—thus stood we silent opposite each other,—
How long; . . . . ."

This choice must be considered more fortunate
than Kaulbach's—who selected the scene, poor in
action, in which the Queen asks heaven to reconcile
the hostile brothers. It afforded Jaeger an opportunity to furnish a picture full of grace and freshness
from this otherwise dull tragedy. Attractive and
full of womanly gracefulness is Beatrice,—before her
stands lively and full of youthful arrogance Don
Manuel to whose hitherto unbridled passions she
offers a resistance he never knew before. These two
figures present an effective contrast which is still
kept up by the flying fown, and the hound eager
after prey. Regarding the action which so faithfully
reflects the Poet's words, we abstain from any com-
ments. The whole is easily understood. The Roman
dress of Don Manuel, the fire of his eyes, his bushy
black hair, the tropical vegetation, and still more the
peculiar illumination, bear testimony to the inge-
niousness with which the Artist entered into the
spirit of the story.

# WALLENSTEIN.

WALLENSTEIN

# WALLENSTEIN.

This largest and most sublime drama of Schiller, the greatest effort of his genius, is essentially distinguished from his other dramatic productions. The latter may not improperly be called offsprings of his fancy, whereas the trilogy of which this drama is the third part, is the result of his research. Don Carlos, Maria Stuart, Joan of Arc, and Tell, have, indeed, an historical background; but Schiller borrowed the names only, not the characters of his heroes from History; whilst he presents to us in Wallenstein absolutely historical personages. Formerly—so Schiller writes about it "I tried to replace wanting truth by beautiful ideality, as in Posa and Carlos,—here in Wallenstein I will attempt to make amends for the want of ideality by positive truth."

This striving, however, of Schiller after historical truth which grew with him into enthusiasm whilst he was occupied with composing this work—also indicated out the path which the Artist had to strike. A mere illustration to the words would not have been sufficient. The Artist would have run the risk

of representing the actor of the part instead of
Wallenstein himself. Mr. Jaeger escaped this danger
by producing a composition which bears the stamp
of an historical painting, worthy by its monumental
character to adorn the walls of a palace as a fresco.
The vigorous, broad, pithy style of drawing is of a
pleasing effect, because it is entirely in keeping with
the character of that age, and renders the deeply
affecting gravity of the represented scene so much
more conspicuous. There is no figure wanting, none
to which we should like another place assigned. Even
the many subordinate objects—as the chandelier hanging down from the ceiling, or the hat and sword
of Illo, rather tend to enhance the total impression
than to impair it.

The action itself is too well known to require
any particular explanation. The scene is at the close
of the fourth act, and represents Max Piccolomini,
after manfully struggling between duty and love,
yielding to the latter, and thereby preparing for
himself an early death before the enemy.

"You have chosen to your own destruction;—
Who follows me, must be prepared to die!"

are the words he calls to the Pappenheim cuirassiers
who had pressed into the ducal chamber to deliver
their Colonel from the hands of the apostate leader
of the Catholic army. They are magnificent figures,
these Pappenheimers,—iron like their age and ar-
mour. To Piccolomini's youthful enthusiasm the
mour and motionless figure of the Duke forms a

striking contrast, and renders him—as in the drama, so here in the illustration—the chief person. His resolution is not to be shaken, even not by the imploring words of his sister. But his countenance betrays the bitter disappointment he feels by the loss of his dearest friend. He seems to have some foreboding that with Max fortune has forsaken him. But he is in the iron grasp of ambition and offended pride, and thus prevented from choosing the better and safer way. How touching is, on the other hand, the tender affection of the mother, the Duchess, which urges her to hasten to the assistance of her daughter who is about to faint in the bitter pangs of her heart; whilst Illo and Terzky follow the faithless leader with looks of indignation and hatred.

# The Maiden's Lament.

6*

THE MAIDEN'S LAMENT

# The Maiden's Lament.

The poet and the artist introduce us here to a com-
bat of the elements. Here we hear the groans of the
old oak-trees; yonder the angry waves, lashing the
rocky shore. The heaven is dark and threatening,
occasionally relieved by vivid flashes of lightning.
The bird seeks the secure shelter of its nest, the
beast of the forest its den. Man alone seems regard-
less of the mighty commotion, when his heart is
bleeding in bitterest sorrow: and both words and
tears are all expended in testimony of his unutter-
able woe. In such a state he leaves his narrow
home, and finds his language in the howling of
the tempest, the roaring of the waves which
silence the anguish of the soul, direct the eyes to
heaven, seeking from there consolation.—And presently the dark clouds disperse, a bright star
arises in the horizon—whispering to the despairing heart: "that beyond the sky the lost ones
live; and that he will soon there join them."— Near
the sea-shore we notice a Maiden, her aching head
pressed in her hand. She has no more tears for the

lover whom yonder treacherous waves engulfed.
From this spot she waved the last parting kiss to
him, whom stern duty called away from her side.
Here she had many a day anxiously looked for the
flag so dear to her; and here it was that on a night
like the present she heard the alarm-guns of a dis-
tressed crew amidst the roaring thunder; and here
again in the morning following this disastrous night
—the waves now pacified brought near the shore
the wrecks of the lost ship—together with the cruel
tidings of lost happiness. Many a day did the dis-
consolate Maiden resort to this place, weep long and
bitterly, until her eyes now dim with tears, no longer wept—and she in blank despair accused high
heaven of having not only robbed her of her earthly
bliss—but in her misery refused her consolation.
But on this day she meditates upon the happiness
once her own—the pleasant hours which passed
away at her lover's side.—Peace visits the troubled
soul and gratefully she turns her eyes to heaven, in
recognition of past happiness.

Thus calmed she repeats in silence:

> "Let flow the useless course of tears,
> No mourning will arouse the dead!—
> The truest balm for a bleeding heart—
> After the joys of sweetest love—
> Are the pains and wailings of love!"

# The Youth at the Brook.

THE YOUTH AT THE BROOK

# THE YOUTH AT THE BROOK.

Schiller's immortal genius presented the world with two jewels, in composing the highly tragic epic— the Maiden's lament—and the pretty idyl entitled as above. It is no mere accident which placed these poems in Schiller's works side by side. They are parts of a great picture, descriptive of the sad commencement, and the tragical termination of love. In the former we pity the mourner whose hopes are laid in the tomb from where there is no return. Here we sympathize with the fate of a youth, striving after the possession of a happiness almost beyond his reach; and whose otherwise joyous springtime is clouded with a great sorrow. The Maiden's lament is lost in the contest of the elements—but here, above the thousand voices of nature resounds the yearning Adagio of the Youth at the Brook. Like Jaeger in the former illustration, so here Pixis succeeded admirably in relating the story which the few verses of Schiller suggest in one single figure. Here sits the youth near the rushing brook, his sorrowful countenance bespeaks his troubled heart.

7

Opposite to him, on an almost inaccessible rock is
the proud castle of the Baron, in whose splendid
apartments the loved one dwells.   Here on the out-
skirts of the wood stands the youth's entire fortune
—a little hut—his sole inheritance.   He is unable to
offer the Lady anything beyond a faithful heart
and a strong arm—but will that propitiate the pride
of the noble father?—He can never hope to win the
prize.   He looks out for messengers that shall at
least tell the fair one of his love, that she may know
what makes his days so sad, his nights so restless.
He gathers the choicest flowers of spring which grow
near him in the shade of the beech-trees, to bind a
fragrant wreath; but despairing of success with such
a trifling gift he drops them one by one into the
rushing brook,—all, but the rose, the emblem of fer-
vent love.   This flower—he says—shall wither in her
hand and tell her what these lips may not utter.
Perhaps the rose will move her heart, and she will
follow me in God's free nature, where thousand
voices sing of love; where thousands of flowers adorn
her path—and she will soon forget her father's castle
content and happy by my side, for:

> "There is room enough in the smallest hut
> For a happy, loving pair!"

# THE PLAYING INFANT.

.

THE PLAYING INFANT

# THE PLAYING INFANT.

One of the best of German authors, Jean Paul, says:
"There are three roads leading to happiness. The
first going upwards, is: to ascend far above the
clouds of life, so that the external world with its
numerous pitfalls, its charnel-houses &c.—appears
deep below our feet not larger than a tiny garden.
The second is: to drop straight down into this little
garden, and to make one's abode so homely in a
furrow, that, in looking out of this snug lark's nest,
one sees also nothing of the world's pitfalls and
charnel-houses, but only the golden ears of corn.
The third is: to use the two alternately." This latter
road Art is to show us. Schiller well understood how to
draw beautiful pictures of everyday life, and exhibit
them by the magic lantern of his poesy in their
rosiest hues. This little poem belongs to that class
in which the poet, true to the description of his con-
temporaries—appears as a highly amiable man. It
was necessary for the artist who engaged to produce
an illustration to these verses to know, like the
poet, how to speak to our hearts. He has well

acquitted himself of the task. We are introduced into
such a little garden, where a happy couple far away
from the noise and bustle of the great world, have
their habitation. The old hunting-lodge in the midst
of the forest affords no prospect,—it is a little world
in itself. When the ordinary duties of the Forester
call him from home, his young and handsome wife
visits a favorite spot not far away, and resting on
a mossy stone beside the rustling brook, playing
with her little son, forgets care and sorrow—which
steal into every home—in a mother's joy and happiness. When late in the day the father returns he
loves to watch his wife and child and silently thanks
heaven, which in return for honest toil has blessed
him with quiet domestic happiness. He smiles at
the zeal of his little son who tries to imitate his
father in his occupation:—for children love to do so,
—not knowing or even caring to know the object
of it.—Perhaps the father thinks of the time when
this happy boy of his must face the world and enter
upon the serious business of life,—when he, despairing of success, will often with disgust fulfil the duties of a station chosen by himself. Therefore he
grudges not the boy the short and happy time of
innocent pleasure; and calls to him:

"Play, my boy, for soon enough thy work commences,
The arduous and serious task of life,
And to comply with the demands of duty
Both inclination and courage often fail!"

# EXPECTATION.

EXPECTATION

# EXPECTATION.

In the biographies of Schiller we find no distinct allusion to the love by which that cycle of poems was caused which begin the so-called third period. We may, however, justly assume that they were not addressed to a mere ideal. The anxious doubt between hope and fear described in this poem, the various delusions in which an excited imagination indulges, were evidently penned under the impression of what actually happened. That the Lady who had gained the affection of the poet—already a middle-aged man—belonged to the upper circle of society, his two other poems, the "Meeting" and the "Secret", remove every doubt. From this point of view the subject was conceived by the artist who undertook to portray the moment in which the expectant lover is relieved of his uncertainty.

> "And softly, as if coming from celestial heights,
> The hour of bliss appears."

We recognise in the picture—though the artist no doubt intentionally avoided a strict resemblance —the poet himself, seated on a stone bench in a vine-arbour, through whose leaves the silvery moon-

8

light softly steals. His weary head has sunk upon
his right hand, whilst the left rests carelessly on the
back of his seat. The half-closed eyes betray a state,
preceding slumber and always following the disappointment of high expectations. To this melancholy
figure the object of his love forms a most effectual
contrast. Frolic, cheerfulness and love—and even some
pity for the sufferer whose patience had been sorely
tried, are reflected in her pretty face. Over the
whole appearance of the Lady a grace and loveliness are effused which fully comment on the feelings
of the poet.

> "Thus did she appear unseen,—
> And aroused by her kisses the friend!"

Yet not without a little roguery is this accomplished, for she first gently touches the cheek turned
away from her, in order to make the slumberer turn
to the side where she is not. In calling attention
to the delicate features of this easily intelligible composition, and the full comprehension of the poem by
the artist, we must also point out the high technical
merit of the picture. How successfully, for example,
has the moonlight been represented; the beautiful fountain and every part of the personal attire
especially the delicate veil which, instead of a warm
neckerchief Schiller's beloved has carelessly bound
round her neck. Every leaf of the arbour, and every
fold of the dress evince an equal care and most
admirable finish—which render this illustration one of
the most successful of this work.

# THE MAIDEN FROM AFAR.

8*

THE MAIDEN FROM AFAR

# THE MAIDEN FROM AFAR.

The well-known Artist, an ever welcome guest to
high circles, and consequently familiar with high-life,
has shown his masterly skill in depicting the domestic life of the upper classes in a very attractive
manner. In this picture, however, he tried to represent an absolutely ideal figure. The task was so
much more difficult, as scarcely with any show of dis-
tinctness can be said, whom or what the Poet meant
by the Maiden from afar. The poem itself seems
to indicate that Poesy was meant;—Apollo also made
his appearance first to shepherds;—the third verse:

> "Her presence gladdened every heart,
> And widened every breast.
> But her dignity and loftiness
> Prevented familiarity"

appears even to justify such supposition. However,
the beginning of the poem which designates Spring
as the usual time of the Maiden's appearance, would
not be consistent with that conjecture. No doubt,
when Spring awakes nature from her winter sleep

the heart of man is likewise filled with joyful agita-
tion; it is better fitted for accepting of what is good
and beautiful and consequently more susceptible to
the noble gifts of poesy. But this feeling does not
die with Spring and even not when earth again has
donned her sombre dress. Poesy is not bound to
place or time. Others thought the Maiden to be
Spring itself. However, Spring has no fruits to dis-
pense. The nearest approach to right interpretation
may, perhaps be, taking the mysterious being for
the embodied Joy of life. It revives in Spring, fills
the old man's heart with youthful desires, the vigorous man's with new hopes, and arrives at its climax
in juvenile souls to which, for the first time, the
paradise of love is opened.

As the Poet has left the interpretation of his
Maiden to our own imagination,—so also the Artist
will not impose his opinion upon us by investing the
figure with any distinguishing attribute. He contents
himself with presenting to us a female endowed with
every grace—the kind fairy of the fable, wandering
through the valley with bounteous hands. Her heavenly appearance is still more favourably set off by
the buxom country-lass and the smart lad who look
up to the divine figure with awe and joy. When the
Artist borrowed the scenery from the Bavarian High-
lands, as it seems indicated by the thatching of the
huts, peculiar to that country, his object undoubtedly
was to render the foreign aspect of the maiden
whose antique attire would by no means be surpris-

ing in a classic landscape, more conspicuous and
effective. But in doing so he at the same time came
nearer to Schiller's intention who did not wish us
to recognise in this maiden an inmate of Olympus
but an Ideal living and working in our mind even
at the present time.

# The Song of the Bell.

# The Song of the Bell.

INTRODUCTION.

On a fine morning in the year 1799, the master bell-founder of Apolda near Jena, was aroused from the attention with which he watched the progress of the melting bell-metal in the furnace,—preparatory to the casting of a new bell for the principal church of the capital,—by a pleasing voice exclaiming: "Good day to you, master! may I come in?" At the salutation of the stranger the bell-founder turned from the furnace, and approached the visitor bare-headed, offering to shake hands. "Welcome to you, Sir"— replied the master. "I could not have a better omen for the success of my casting, than the arrival of you, heaven's favorite." The stranger was 'Friedrich Schiller',—who, tempted by the beautiful weather, had taken a walk from Jena to Apolda. In spite of his guest's attempt to prevent, the bell-founder summoned his daughter to prepare some refreshment for his welcome visitor. Soon Wilhelmina appeared with the best the house could afford, placed it before Schiller whom she greeted with unaffected pleasure;

9*

yet also with an expression of profound respect.
The works of the poet she kept together with other
treasures, elegantly bound in a glass case. "A charming girl"—observed Schiller—when she had left the
room. "She is that"—replied the father—"pretty and
good, like her departed mother. I should not know
what to do without her." "Then, rejoined the poet,
she will make some day an excellent wife. Has some
future son-in-law already announced himself?" "Pro-
fessor, replied smilingly the father, young people
have always some secret game behind the backs of
their parents, and we must patiently await the issue."
"And have you noticed anything of the kind?"
"Well—yes! The foreman yonder, a brave and
honest young man, and a relative of mine. He
possesses a small inheritance, which, together with
what I am able to leave my daughter, will suffice
to keep them from want; and enable him to carry
on the business as a respectable citizen." 'Please,
Master',—called one of the workmen from near the
furnace. The bellfounder hastened to give advice
and assistance in the important work in hand.
Meanwhile Schiller had turned his eyes through the
open door upon the scenes of the street. The curl-
ing smoke from numerous chimneys proclaimed the
approach of the dinner hour;—the merry voices of
children returning from school greeted his ears.
They seemed to seek in their innocent mirth some
compensation for the restraint which the school hours
imposed. Presently another sight presented itself.

A wanderer dusty and tired emerged from a narrow
street,—a youth with blue eyes, and curly fair hair.
He carried in his hand a stout stick, and a well
supplied knapsak on his back. He approached the
workshop and inquired for the master. Announcing
himself a fellow-craftsman, he asked for employment.
Schiller was attracted by the voice of the stranger,
and recognised with pleasure his native dialect. He
warmly grasped the hand of the youth, and offered
him the glass of wine intended for himself. After
a short interrogation the stranger was installed a
fellow-workman. During these transactions the heart
of Schiller had been powerfully stirred. The sweet
pictures of his own home appeared before his mind.
He seemed to recognise in the little town of Apolda
his own native Marbach;—the gentle hills of the
valley of the Saal reminded him of the rough moun-
tains of the Suabian Alps. The thought of his dear
mother filled him with tender emotions. He remembered his sister, whom he left a child, and who must
now have grown into womanhood. He remembered
the time when he, obedient to the call of the Muses,
had secretly made his escape from Stuttgart—poor
in pocket, rich in hopes.—His friendly reception at
Karlsruhe, his quiet happiness at Bauerbach, and his
first success at Leipzig,—all these various pictures
of the past, one after another, appeared before his
mind's eye.—He was reminded of manifold sorrows
and hardships too; but could also with grateful
modesty acknowledge: That he had not in vain striv-

en after his high object, that his hopes had been
realised: he was honored and loved as a teacher,
a celebrated poet, a happy husband and father. It
was the life of man—much tried, much agitated,—
which was passing before his mind. Greatly moved
he took out his pocket-book and pencil, and depicted life with all its joys and sorrows, with its hopes
and disappointments; and presented us with an effu-
sion from our own souls, calling it:

"The song of the Bell."

# MOTHER'S LOVE.

MOTHER'S LOVE

# MOTHER'S LOVE.

There he is lying and kicking about, the little darling, naked as in the hour of his birth; his future still wrapped in darkness. Life appears to him in rosiest hues. It resembles the spring morning, the warm rays of whose sun are softly stealing through the round panes of the window into the homely room. It is certainly a comfortable nest, in which the little citizen of the world has been born. The offspring of well-to-do people, to judge by the condition of the chamber which has everywhere the appearance of comfort and neatness. Even the fat bullfinch on the top of its cage proves that here no pressing want stunts the joy of childhood. With what a happy face the mother looks at her darling! How carefully does she now lift the napkin, and then again quickly drop it on him; for she is playing with her dearest one at hide and seek.— How perfectly acquainted she is with all his wants, and how eager to satisfy them. Hunger will very soon start the first tears; but her half uncovered bosom shows that she has thought of it. Washing

over, she will nurse him at her breast. And when
by degrees the little eyes become heavy, she will
put him in his cradle, and lull him to rest,—but her
loving gaze will still rest on the slumberer, and a
happy dream may yet keep the dear face before him.
Even as Schiller in the few words:

"The mother's love, and tender care,
Watch o'er his golden morning"; —

describes a mother's affection and joy,—so the Artist has portrayed in the two figures all the feelings
of the heart of that happy one whom heaven has
blessed with its choicest gift of matrimony. And not
only will mothers gaze with pleasure at the lovely
picture,—the man also, whose heart has been harden-
ed by the storms of life, will silently contemplate the
scene, and perchance think of the mother long ago
laid in the silent tomb.—It will become a household-
picture, to which the father will lead his son, should
he forget his mother's wishes and injunctions,—and
will say to him: "See, my son, thus your mother
with true affection, tended you, when, a helpless child,
you were lying in your cradle."

# THE FAREWELL.

10*

THE FAREWELL

# The Farewell.

The ardent wish of the mother, that heaven would bless her with more children, has not been fulfilled. Hence the little fellow whom we saw cushioned in the previous picture, has for many a year to amuse himself alone; until the father adopted a poor orphan cousin as his own child. After the first natural shyness has worn off, the children become fervently attached to each other. They share their little joys and sorrows, and seem inseparable. By and by the time comes, when the boy must attend school; and Mary is full of joy when some time afterwards she is allowed to accompany her elder brother. He would assist her in her lessons, and she, in return, does everything to please him. In the course of time Mary has to aid her mother in her household duties,—whilst the boy, in a higher school, is sorely troubled with syntax and Cornelius Nepos. Mary would still continue to meet her brother on his way from school, and attend to his wishes at home. But some change has come over him. The boy seems no longer grateful for the attention of his

adopted sister and not unfrequently repays it by
wanton raillery. He would appear at times to
be ashamed of her society; and a feeling of sad-
ness comes over the girl. Yet she still hopes to
regain the old affection, but in vain. The strict
discipline of school allows no other outlet to his
exuberant boyish temper. than teasing his good-
natured sister. And how the boy hates this re-
striction which appears to destroy every germ of
awaking independance! How he longs to be free,
to wander unrestrained in the world! Whenever
he stood upon the neighbouring heights and
gazed upon the distant hills, behind which the spires
of several churches were visible—he would think
of a different people, dwelling there, accustomed to
modes of life other than his own. To-day at last his
wish has been fulfilled, and he is obout to start on his
journey, his own master, no longer under an irksome
restraint. Although he has anxiously looked forward
to this day, his heart is heavy, when, on parting,
he promises to foliow his fathers advice. And when
he offers a farewell kiss to his mother he weeps
aloud. But he tears himself from her embrace, and
dries his last tear. The mother's heart is almost
broken with anxiety and sorrow; but the father
looks with pride upon his son, and tries to comfort
her, saying: "He will keep his promise." On
taking leave of his early playmate Mary, his former
cheerfulness revives; and he endeavours to hide his
emotions under good-natured jokes, when he observes

the tears in Mary's eyes. Even now he shows no
gratitude; he has not a word of affection for the sorrowing maiden; but

"Vom Maedchen reisst sich stolz der Knabe."

It is not tillin after years, when he stands
alone in the world, when many hopes have been
disappointed, when he is troubled with want and
care,—that he thinks of her, and repents of his cold-
ness in return for her sisterly affection. Although
the Artist depicts a time when patriarchal customs
still prevailed,—he has nevertheless presented to
us a picture from our own life. Men will re-
collect the high expectations with which they set
out upon their journey of life, when they first left
the paternal roof. Mothers will think of the absent
ones, alone to battle with the adversities of life.
May they never do so with a feeling of grief!

# The Return.

THE RETURN

# The Return.

The Artist presents to us again a charming picture of simple family-life. The little snug oriel is known to us as the favorite place of the father where, after the day's labour he enjoys a quiet hour with his family. It is Sunday to day, as may be seen by the broad cloth frock and neat white cap of the mother, and the fresh flowers with which Mary has adorned the Crucifix. Supper is just over, but the snow-white table cloth has not yet been removed. "I wonder, observes the mother—if our absent son has enjoyed his meals to-day?"—and she casts a sad glance upon the vacant place, formerly occupied by him. She thinks with a sigh of the many years he has been away. The father smiling at the question of the mother, relates some merry story from his own time when he was sowing his wild oats, to assure the sorrowing mother that young people rarely suffer want—even when purse and knapsack are well nigh empty. On this occasion he praises the time of this own early life, when young men had more spirit than now, he called t, as usual, 'the good old time'.

11*

In compliance with ancient usage, the father desires
Mary to read a prayer from the prayer book; to
which he listens with becoming earnestness, but also
with the satisfaction of a man who can say that
he has spent his life well, and attained what he
aimed at. But the modest mother includes in the
prayer her good wishes for her absent child. The
dog "Spitz", acquainted with the rules of the house,
listens with as much attention as a dog is capable of,
he is even angrily snapping at a fly, which by its
buzzing interrupts the stillness. But now he hears
suddenly quick approaching steps, and jumps towards
the door, through which at the same moment a tall
youth enters. Who could recognise in the stately
figure, in the manly, handsome face of the traveller,
the beloved son? Nobody believed him to be so near;
for in his last letter there was no intimation of his
return. The neighbours could not have recognised him,
for none had greeted him. The servants of the house
followed him silently with their looks, not knowing
who he was. And now on entering the dear old room,
he is received by the savage barking of 'Spitz'.
Even his own father looks almost angrily upon the
intruder who dares disturb them in their prayers
—for

"Fremd kehrt er heim in's Vaterhaus."

But no! The foreboding heart of the mother tells
her who he is, and she hastens to press the returned
wanderer to her heart. The two most precious tears
sparkle in her eyes—those of a mothers happiness,

and a mother's pride. There in the corner of the
room stands Mary. She also has recognised him at
once. With her eye cast down she silently awaits
his greeting; for she does not think it becoming a
maid to make advances towards a young man. He
will do so, but full of astonishment he stops. Is that
the same Mary, the little chubby girl he had left?

> "Und herrlich, in der Jugend Prangen,
> Wie ein Gebild aus Himmelshoeh'n,
> Mit zuechtigen. verschaemten Wangen
> Sieht er die Jungfrau vor sich steh'n."

He forgets his usual bantering tone in which he
formerly had spoken to her; and released from his
mothers embrace, and after having heartily shaken
his father by the hand, he timidly approaches Mary.
He can utter in a faltering voice only a few polite
words—he hardly ventures to look into her eyes or
seize her hands. His former arrogance has disap-
peared.

# COURTSHIP.

COURTSHIP

# COURTSHIP.

Mary probably understood why the greeting of her cousin on his return was so very polite, and no longer so warm as in former times, for even an innocent girl has a quick perception in such matters. Now the time had come when she might effectually punish him for his former petulancy, and, as all revenge is sweet, she tormented him to her hearts desire. When he endeavoured to be amiable, she would be perverse; when he was civil, she would appear formal, when he sighed, she laughed at him and rendered his heavy heart still heavier. But so it has been always. Women wish to be won. Our friend was subject to the common lot. The day which brought him safely back to his father's house, revealed to him the beauty and virtues of his cousin Mary. Her possession would make him extremely happy. But how could he obtain this treasure? In his wanderings he had greeted many a damsel, and received many a smile in return, but with Mary he could never succeed. When he wished to converse with

her, his eyes were pensively fixed upon her, but his
tongue remained silent, for he pictured to himself his
happiness at her side, built many castles in the air, till
Mary at last would arise and dash them down with the
remark: "Well, cousin, to-day you have been again
very entertaining." This would make him very un-
happy, he would reproach himself with want of courage, and resolve on the next occasion to ask frankly
the all-important question. Alas! the time came, and
once more his courage failed. He had moreover
nobody in whom he could confide, or ask counsel of.
From his friends he feared ridicule; from his father
almost reproaches; and in the trusty counsel of
his mother he had not sufficient confidence, fearing
she might interpret his sufferings as idle thoughts.
Again it is Sunday. His young companions have
invited him to some rural feast, but their mirth and
noise annoy him. He wishes to be alone with his
sorrow. He longs for solitude. In the fields and
woods, through which he directs his weary steps,
everywhere above and below, he hears signs of joy
and love, and should he be a solitary mourner?—No,
he would not let the day pass without having de-
clared his love. He had often prepared speeches and
selected poetry in which he hoped to convey his
passion; but whenever he was in the presence of
Mary, he seemed altogether unable to utter a word.
Presently his searching eye lights upon the flowery
meadow, and he sees himself helped out of his dis-
tress:

"Das Schoenste sucht er auf den Fluren,
Womit er seine Liebe schmueckt!"

The flowers shall speak in his behalf and inform
Mary of what he endures for her sake. Should she
accept the trifling gift, he would be assured, that his
hopes have not deceived him. And straightway he
hastens to his father's garden, where he knows he
will find Mary alone to-day. At sight of her, he hides
himself behind a tree; he is greatly agitated, he
hesitates. Presently he hears Mary, unconscious of
his presence, softly utter his name, not in derision
or ridicule. This encourages him to emerge from
his hiding-place, and with the bunch of flowers in
his extended hand, he sinks at her feet asking:
„Mary will you be mine?"

12*

# HAPPY MOMENTS.

HAPPY MOMENTS

# Happy Moments.

This is a picture in which the Artist has put all the poetical sweetness, all the tender pathos of Schiller's words:

> "O zarte Sehnsucht, suesses Hoffen!
> Der ersten Liebe gold'ne Zeit!
> Das Auge sieht den Himmel offen,
> Es schwelgt das Herz in Seligkeit;
> O, dass sie ewig gruenen bliebe,
> Die schoene Zeit der jungen Liebe!"

with so much delicacy of feeling and consummate beauty, that the observer must feel affected with deep emotion. There is nothing trite, and yet nothing strange in it. It is the ideal of happiness; the high festival of the soul, such as we picture or have pictured to ourselves. The lovely landscape which is in perfect harmony with the scene, the exquisite drapery of these handsome, peaceful figures, the wreath of flowers in the hair of the maiden everything shows an equal warmth of conception, and an equally elaborate manner of treatment. Indeed, no suitor will for the future be at a loss, like our friend, for means to express his love. He will simply present to the object of his affection this picture, and say:

"Let us be as happy as they are." And there is but little fear that a request thus made, will meet with a refusal: Mary too, could not find it in her heart to torment her cousin any longer. To be sure, girls have many an 'if' and 'but', as a last resort in a siege, ere they unconditionally surrender to the beloved enemy. But no seeming obstacles will daunt a resolute suitor; for they may easily be removed. That Mary's near relationship cannot be any hindrance, he clarly proves by citing similar unions—her scruple about her poverty, he will not entertain—and her apprehension that his parents will withhold their consent to the union on account of that poverty, he simply refutes by leading Mary to them. The day on which the father's consent and blessing have been obtained, and the good mother with tears of joy has embraced her happy children; the pair are walking proudly and openly for the first time, arm in arm, through the streets. They heed not the idle gossip of curious friends and neighbours; but ascend the hill from which the boy had years ago so longingly gazed on the wide world. He no longer desires to roam about; his own home has become more than ever dear to him. The happiness he sought among strangers in vain, he found at the side of Mary. The girl that he once left with such an easy heart, has opened for him the gates of heaven on earth; and in the consciousness of his happiness he said gratefully to her: "Mary, I shall never leave you again, I will always love you."

# THE BRIDAL PROCESSION.

THE BRIDAL PROCESSION

# The Bridal Procession.

Although it is very likely that not a few fond
mothers may have secretly envied Mary's happiness,
for the sake of their own daughters; still on this day,
when Mary follows her bridegroom to the altar, all
signs of jealousy disappear. On her stepping forth,
beaming with joy and beauty, all evil tongues are
silent. Words only in praise of her exquisite dress,
her trinkets, nay even of her virtue are heard.—
Love generally commences in stillness and secrecy,
but likes to have its sacred bonds tied openly and
solemnly. The marriage-day is the true festival of
life, and here the happy bridegroom is greeted
with kind words and wishes from all. Friends have
secretly adorned the hall of the house and the companions of the bride have embroidered the piece of car-
pet for them to kneel on at the altar. The father and
mother appear young again in the prospect of happiness for their son, and live their own wedding-day
over once more. Curiosity has attracted a crowd of
neighbours. Children have for a while forsaken their
play, and are strewing flowers along the path the happy

13*

pair must tread; and when the procession has entered
the church they will in their own childlike way play
bride and bridegroom. The little girl leaning over the
rails so far that her pretended husband is obliged to
hold her, has already adorned herself with a crown.
Every one present is greatly interested in the pro-
ceeding, and no signs of impatience are visible. At
last the musicians, heading the procession, strike up,
followed by the bridegroom, leading Mary by the
hand. They are hailed with loud and joyous shouting.
Of all the beautiful maids that accompany her, she
is the most beautiful. Splendid is her dress, costly
her golden girdle and crown, an heirloom of the
family of which she has become a member; grace-
ful is her carriage and gait, and:

> "Lieblich in der Braeute Locken
> Spielt der jungfraeuliche Kranz,
> Wenn die hellen Kirchenglocken
> Laden zu des Festes Glanz."

We can hardly fancy a more beautiful memorial
of the bridal day than this cheerful, well-conceived
picture of the artist Mueller, in which mirth and earnestness are blended, as on the day whose celebration
it represents. Happy that couple who can say when
looking at this picture in after years: "The hopes
we then cherished have not been disappointed."

# THE MOTHER'S CARES.

THE MOTHERS CARES

# THE MOTHER'S CARES.

"Und drinnen waltet
Die znechtige Hausfrau,
Die Mutter der Kinder
Und herrschet weise
Im haeuslichen Kreise,
Und lehret die Maedchen,
Und wehret den Knaben —"

Once more we cast our eyes upon Mary, but no
longer the petulant girl of former days, nor the
happy bride. Many years have passed away, and
Mary is a mother. However, she has preserved her
cheerful disposition and loveliness,—though just now
her brow is knit in looking at the little 'good for
nothing' who has taken his sister's pear, and con-
cales his face behind the picture-book. He does perhaps not wish his mother to see that he is just now
commencing to eat the stolen pear—or, will he first
taste the sweetness of the fruit ere the rod, hanging
at the back of his mother's chair is felt? It is pos-

sible, for just now the little sister says with a
troubled countenance: "Mamma, Max has taken my
pear!" But his whole punishment will propably be,
that he gets no lunch to-day. Sad enough for him,
since he thought to have earned it by teaching his
younger brother the A, B, C,—and had already
come as far as the second letter of the alphabet.
The tasks of the elder sisters are not quite so easy.
The eldest a striking resemblance to the mother, has
just finished hemming a cloth, and fetches another
for which she looks for room on the table where
the mother has laid a heavy silk bed-cover, which
is to replace the old one upon the bed of the father,
for:

> "Und fueget zum Guten den Glanz und den Schimmer."

Opposite the mother sits the second daughter,
busily engaged in knitting. She glances at Max with
a look that seems to say: "A good flogging would
do you no harm, for you are always naughty." And
what shall we say of the little one, who so content-
edly sits upon his cushion on the floor? He also
has fairly earned his lunch, for it was no little
trouble to cause such topsy-turvy state of a whole
town and soldiers and horses; besides the work of
sounding a bell, and rolling a large ball about the
room. Well, for all this labour the nurse will
presently bring him a bowl of warm milk. On
taking leave of this peaceful work-room, we must
acknowledge that the mother knows well how

to make home truly happy and attractive. How
bright and clean is every thing, not a particle of
dust on the floor, no spot upon the dresses is per-
mitted; and the open linen-press shows, that the
ample store which a kind aunt had given her on her
wedding day, has not only been preserved, but
largely increased.

# HARVEST-HOME.

14*

HARVEST HOME

# HARVEST-HOME.

Schiller after having represented in the first part
of his Lay of the Bell the life of an individual, turns
in the second part to the life of the people, and
shows us the bright and the dark side of it. The
consequence was that the Artist was obliged to drop
figures that had become familiar, and even dear to
us, and to pass from representing the quiet of domestic life to picturing the lively stir of the people.
The two young girls only, looking on so wistfully at
the dancing, remind us of Mary, now a sedate house-
wife. They would surely join the merry dancers,
were not the "careful aunt", that inevitable appen-
dage to every respectable family, standing behind
them as an unseasonable check. But all the people
here are strangers to us, except the fiddler, an old
acquaintance of ours, who headed Mary's bridal procession; and who, in spite of his old age, appears as
full of merry tricks as his neighbour, the piper.
Perhaps he anticipates the pleasure of being present at the wedding which that dancing couple be-
before him may celebrate some day. For do not

their faces speak of happiness, as if all these doings
around them were already now going on in honour
of them; though their love may be of no longer
standing than since the last harvesting. There is a
jolly time now down in the dry moat of the old
town, in the shade of mighty linden. The returning
herd is just passing by, and the young herdsman
and an inquisitive goat show more interest in what
is going on, than the respectable looking townsmen
who calculate with a knowing eye the value of the
last laden cart. They are evidently two magistrates,
representatives of that "eye of the Law" that watch-
es over the weal and woe of the inhabitants and
their own.—Thus Mueller has compressed the whole
verse of Schiller into this picture. By doing so, the
place for dancing has certainly turned out a little
small; and our modern dancers would scarcely put
up with it. However, it was still the "good, old
time", when all were moving in a small compass;—
why not also in a narrow dancing place?

# SCHILLER AT WEIMAR.

SCHILLER IN WEIMAR

# SCHILLER AT WEIMAR.

Kaulbach, as well as Lindenschmit represent both the Poets in the act of celebrating triumphs. But Goethe, the favourite of the Muses, and the spoiled child of fortune, could feel himself as victor only in the midst of storming applause, in the circle of a society to which ordinary people had no admittance. He looked upon the admiration of the multitude as a tribute only due to him. Kaulbach, therefore, selected the scene, when Corona Schroeter, still clad as Iphigenia, crowns the Poet of Tragedy with laurel, in the presence of the applauding Court. Whereas Schiller obliged to climb the rugged, steep road from a military surgeon to a favourite of the German nation, saw his greatest triumph in the esteem of the most eminent men and women of his time, and still more in the domestic happiness at the side of his excellent wife.

Some of his happiest hours he enjoyed at Weimar where he moved to in 1799. Here on every Wednes day afternoon, surrounded by his friends, he could read to them whatever news the Muse had

presented him with.—It is such a meeting Lindenschmit
preferred as a subject for his composition.—Above
Schiller, Musaeus is seen leaning over the balustrade.
Carl August, and Wilhelm v. Humboldt are approaching.    Before them is a very attractive group of
ladies.    Corona Schroeter, the celebrated actress, is
standing behind Frau v. Laroche who had gained
some renown in German Literature, and whose acquaintance Schiller had already made when at
Mannheim.    On her left side Charlotte v. Kalb is
sitting, the reconciled friend of our Poet;—a lady to
whom during his first stay at Weimar, he bore as
tender a love as Goethe to Frau v. Stein.    This in-
timacy, however, was, undoubtedly to Schiller's ad-
vantage, interrupted by Charlotte v. Lengefeld, who
now, a kind hostess, is sitting at the table.    Her
head is lightly resting upon her arm; her eldest boy
in her lap, whilst she looks with pride mingled with
tender care, upon her husband.    Upon her shoulder
is her sister, Frau v. Wolzogen leaning, in the house
of whose mother-in-law at Bauerbach, Schiller met
with the first friendly reception since his escape
from Stuttgart.    There is still another friend at the
table, in the foreground, Frau v. Egloffstein, a com-
panion as spirited, as she was amiable.    It is to
her the Poet seems particularly to address his
words, since he valued her judgment very highly.
Between Schiller's wife and Laroche, Koerner, the
father of Theodor, has found a seat.    He came fre-
quently from Dresden to see his dearest friend.    Be-

hind him Herder and Goethe are standing. The
Artist's reason for not placing them more in the foreground, is to let Schiller to whose memory this
Gallery is dedicated, appear as the only chief figure;
and by doing so the Artist has acquitted himself ho-
nourably of his charge which was, to produce a
counterpart to "Goethe at Weimar."

www.ingramcontent.com/pod-product-compliance
Lightning Source LLC
Chambersburg PA
CBHW030557270326
41927CB00007B/963